GERMS
DISEASE–CAUSING ORGANISMS™

THE FIGHT AGAINST GERMS

MARGAUX BAUM and JOSEPHA SHERMAN

rosen publishing's
rosen central®

Published in 2017 by The Rosen Publishing Group, Inc.
29 East 21st Street, New York, NY 10010

First Edition

Library of Congress Cataloging-in-Publication Data

Names: Baum, Margaux, author. | Sherman, Josepha, author.
Title: The fight against germs / Margaux Baum and Josepha Sherman.
Description: First edition. | New York : Rosen Central, 2017. | Series:
  Germs: disease causing organisms | Audience: Grades 5-8. | Includes
  bibliographical references and index.
Identifiers: LCCN 2016002009| ISBN 9781477788530 (library bound) | ISBN
  9781477788516 (pbk.) | ISBN 9781477788523 (6-pack)
Subjects: LCSH: Bacteria--Juvenile literature.
Classification: LCC QR74.8 .S54 2017 | DDC 579.3--dc23
LC record available at http://lccn.loc.gov/2016002009

Manufactured in China

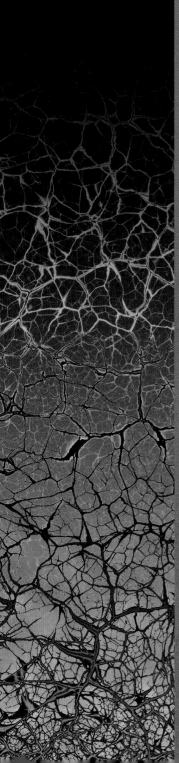

CONTENTS

INTRODUCTION

Think back as early as you can remember. It is likely that at some point in your childhood, your mother or father stopped you from picking up something from the street, or putting something in your mouth. They may have upset you by hurriedly snatching the thing away, while admonishing you, "Don't do that! It's probably covered in germs!"

We use the word "germ" to mean many things. We say we have the germ of an idea, meaning we've come up with the beginning of an idea. But when someone says, "I caught a germ," we instantly know that this means sickness. Germ is the blanket name we use when we refer to bacteria, fungi, microbes, protozoa, viruses, and other disease-causing microorganisms. What all these different types of germs have in common is that they are all very tiny. Unlike other threats to our bodies and health we can easily avoid—such as traffic, an aggressive animal, violent situations—avoiding germs and preventing their spread takes some more thought.

Besides preventing illness on a personal level, society at large, including every civilization that has existed since early human history, has waged a fight against germs in some way, shape, or form. This was true even before people realized the true causes of many illnesses. Even the simplest communities of the ancient world employed measures to prevent the spread of disease-causing germs.

The fight against germs involves both preventive and reactive measures. Scientists and researchers are working now directly to find medical cures for many bacterial and viral infections. Hospitals and other institutions treat those who have fallen ill and set up their physical spaces to prevent illnesses from spreading. Manufacturers make cleaning products that the public buys and uses to clean their homes and cars, as well as hygiene products like soap and antibacterial wipes for personal use.

At the same time, the many different kinds of germs out there are resilient and endlessly adaptable to the various ways that humanity tries to kill or get rid of them. Many other germs are actually beneficial and contribute to human life processes and to the life cycles of the plant and animal life out there—including providing air to breathe, something that all living things depend on for their survival.

Learning about the fight against harmful germs helps us look more closely at a struggle that has occupied humanity for all of its existence. The more we learn about these microscopic creatures, the more we learn about the complex web of relationships that germs and humans are part of.

CHAPTER 1

GERMS: WHAT ARE THEY?

Most of the things we call germs are single-celled (or uni-cellular) organisms, living things whose bodies consist of only one cell apiece. We need microscopes to see them because they are far too small to be seen with the naked eye. Thus, they are known as microorganisms, or microbes. Germs provide a window into the past since they are probably the oldest forms of life on Earth. In fact, some families of germs may have been around for billions of years. They are also probably the most numerous living things on the planet. Today, within our environment and inside us, too, there are almost too many microbes to count. By some estimates, there may be five million trillion trillion bacteria alone! So far, more than four thousand species of just bacteria have been identified and that is likely not the total count.

This overwhelming number of germs shouldn't scare us. Fortunately for most living creatures on Earth, over 95 percent of germs are harmless. Some germs are even "good germs," necessary for animal life. One type of germ, for instance, helps with human digestion. Other types cause the decay of dead plants and animals back into the soil, helping make the soil fertile. Still other types of germs curdle milk into cheese or yogurt. Specialized germs live in the human mouth and fight off disease-causing germs, and even more specialized organisms live at the roots of human eyelashes and keep the lashes clean and healthy.

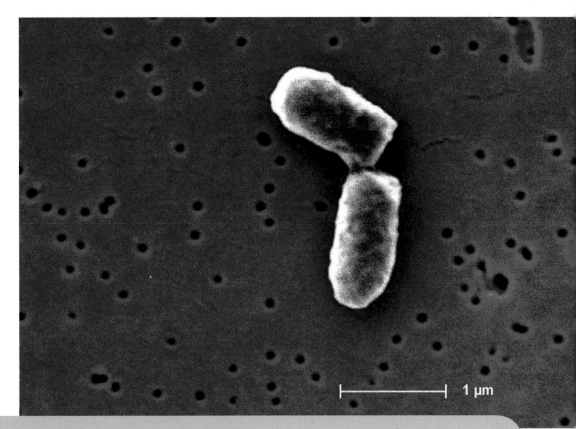

1 µm

A scanning electron micrograph (SEM) provides a close-up of *Escherichia coli*, or *E. coli*, a common bacterium of many animals' digestive systems. Most are harmless, but some *E. coli* strains cause terrible food poisoning.

THE FIGHT AGAINST GERMS

But there are germs that are dangerous—even fatal—to living creatures. Dangerous bacteria cause diseases and problems such as strep throat, pneumonia, diphtheria, and tetanus. They also quickly multiply in improperly cleaned or stored food and cause the unpleasant and sometimes deadly problem called food poisoning. Dangerous viruses can cause diseases like the common cold and influenza—the flu—as well as chicken pox, measles, mumps, and the incurable disease AIDS, which is caused by the human immunodeficiency virus (HIV). Scientists even suspect that some viruses may cause some types of cancer. Protozoa, a diverse group of unicellular life forms with a nucleus, can spread disease through contaminated water. Some protozoa cause intestinal infections leading to pain and diarrhea.

Over the centuries, dangerous germs have killed millions of people. More people died in the Spanish flu epidemic of 1914, which took place during World War I, than were killed in battle in the war. The Black Death, which happened in the fourteenth century, was caused

This engraving depicts the miserable deaths of victims of the bacterial contagion known as *Yersinia pestis* in fourteenth-century Europe, an event known as the Black Death.

by contagious bacteria and killed one-fourth of the population of Europe. Today, people die from AIDS, the flu, and many other diseases that are caused by dangerous germs.

Our bodies have natural defense systems against harmful germs. This is called the immune system, a complicated network of cells and organs that work together. The immune system guards the body against attacks by "foreign" invaders—things it identifies as originating outside the body. Every cell contains specific molecules, tiny bits of matter that identify it as belonging to the body. The immune system normally doesn't attack any cells that have the right identification. Because the immune system doesn't attack those other body cells, it is said that the immune cells and the other body cells keep in a balance known as self-tolerance.

Amazingly enough, the immune system can and will react to millions of foreign germs. It fights them off by creating special substances and cells called antibodies. These antibodies catch and destroy all the outside germs.

While this response is nothing short of wonderful when it comes to fighting off dangerous germs, it can be a problem in the case of an organ transplant. When the immune system identifies transplanted cells as invaders and tries to fight them off, the organ is said to be rejected by the body.

The body has immune organs all through it. These are called lymphoid organs since they create and send out the lymphocytes, or white blood cells, the "warriors" of the immune system.

THE FIGHT AGAINST GERMS

There are several types of white blood cells. The immune system response begins when a type of white blood cell called a macrophage encounters an invading germ and eats it. The macrophage then displays pieces of the "digested" germ on its surface. These pieces of the "dead" virus have now become an antigen. An antigen is anything that triggers the immune system to get to work.

Another type of white blood cell, the helper T cell, identifies the antigen, and the helper T cell joins the macrophage. As they unite, they produce chemicals that allow the white cells to "communicate." This "communication" causes more T cells to be created, both helper T cells and a different type, the killer T cell. As they multiply, the helper T cells also give off chemicals that signal another type of white blood cell, the B cell, to multiply and produce antibodies. Antibodies are substances that fight germs. The B cells release their antibodies, which bind to the germs. The killer T cells punch holes in the germs and any infected cells. Together, these cells kill off the invaders.

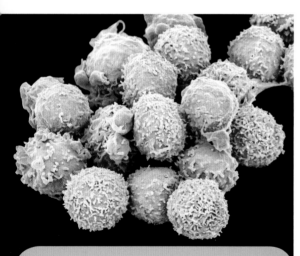

This SEM image of lymphocyte white blood cells shows these crucial helpers of the human immune system nearly three thousand times their actual size.

CONTAGIOUS?

According to the Centers for Disease Control and Prevention (CDC), the U.S. agency that is in charge of protecting the public from disease, the most contagious ailments are among the most common: the common cold and influenza (flu). Flu sufferers can pass their viruses to others within six feet (1.8 meters), as most flu viruses likely travel via droplets in the air—by talking, sneezing, or coughing—though some are spread by casual contact. The flu is contagious about a day before and five days to a week after it starts, while colds can be contagious even a week before people know they're sick and as long as two weeks after onset.

Once the invasion is over, another type of white blood cell, the suppressor T cell, "turns off" the T and B cells. But the system holds on to some "memory cells" so that it can respond more quickly if there's another attack.

There are some basic precautions to defend against germs. Your chance of catching illnesses through casual contact is greatly reduced if you wash your hands regularly with soap and warm water. Properly handling and preparing food also helps. Keeping kitchen counters, cutting boards, knives, and other utensils clean, especially before and after

THE FIGHT AGAINST GERMS

use reduces the chances of spreading foodborne illnesses. So does properly refrigerating and freezing foods and keeping certain foods separate from others—such as making sure poultry and other meats do not potentially contaminate vegetables or other foods. Even just covering your mouth when you sneeze or cough helps when it comes to mitigating the risk of spreading airborne bacterial and viral infections.

Despite taking all possible measures, some germs are dangerous and hardy enough to get through our defenses. It is the fight against these, and humanity's setbacks against them, that have provided some tough lessons.

CHAPTER 2

THE EARLY HISTORY OF THE FIGHT AGAINST GERMS

Today, we take for granted our ability to detect harmful germs using microscopes, blood tests, and other technologies. But it is only recently in human history that we have been fortunate enough to have such tools. The microscope was invented at the end of the sixteenth century. Before that, doctors and scientists had little true knowledge of germs, even if they categorized and treated their effects. All together, the study of the health of human beings and how it is affected by injury and especially disease, is called epidemiology.

MEDICINE IN ANCIENT MESOPOTAMIA

In ancient Mesopotamia (roughly corresponding to modern Syria and Iraq), between 3000 to 1000 BCE, doctors thought that specific gods or demons were responsible for specific diseases. But whatever they thought the cause, doctors worked to find ways to heal diseases and prevent infection. Much of the information about the medicines that they used has been lost, and identifying the different drugs is difficult since there are no translations for the terms the doctors used.

We do know that there were two classes of medical professionals. The first was the *ashipu*, who was responsible for finding out what supernatural force had caused the illness and whether or not the patient had committed any sins. The ashipu was also responsible for any spells or other magics thought necessary. The second medical practitioner was closer to what we think of as a doctor. This was the *asu*. Not only did the asu prescribe medicine, he also knew about the need to keep a wound clean, to wash everything, and to apply clean bandages. An asu also knew how to make a healing plaster out of ingredients that would help fight off infection, and which herbs—such as garlic—had antibiotic or antiseptic uses.

THE ANCIENT EGYPTIANS

Like their counterparts in Mesopotamia, doctors in ancient Egypt didn't know about germs. They also suspected evil supernatural forces were to blame, but that didn't stop them from understanding how to stop infections. We know something about their practices from two doctors' manuals, called by the modern names of the Edwin Smith Papyrus and the Ebers Papyrus.

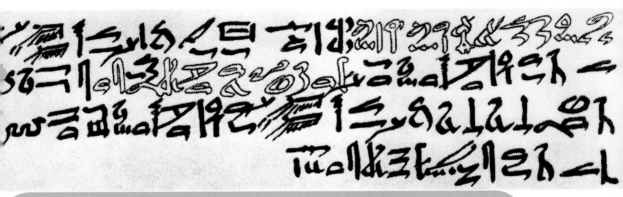

The Ebers Papyrus, estimated to have been written in about 1550 BCE, is shown here. This particular section details a cure for a destructive spell, part of which includes boiling a beetle's wings and head in snake fat.

There were several classes of doctors. What we might call a general practitioner was called a *swnw*, or *sunu*. A doctor who specialized in magic as well as medicine was a *sau*. It was believed that medicine and magic went hand in hand. There were also as many medical specialists in ancient Egypt as there are nowadays, from surgeons to dentists.

To fight infections, Egyptian doctors used antibiotic herbs such as garlic and antiseptics such as oil of fir imported from Palestine. They knew that cleanliness kept away sickness, though not why. One of the most important remedies used to keep wounds free from infection and even scarring was honey. Today, doctors are starting to study the antibiotic properties of honey, which may even be strong enough to kill the toughest germs.

THE FIGHT AGAINST GERMS

While modern researchers are revisiting honey's medicinal qualities, many ancient systems of medicine and healing acknowledged its antimicrobial and curative properties.

GREEK AND ROMAN DIAGNOSES

While the Greeks admitted that the Egyptians were the finest doctors, the Greek doctor Hippocrates, who worked on the island of Kos, is often called the Father of Medicine, mostly because of the more than sixty medical books written by his followers. Hippocrates was the first to state that disease had nothing to do with gods or evil spirits. He separated medicine from religion.

However, his main theory about the human body was incorrect. He said it had four "humors," black bile, yellow bile, phlegm, and blood and stated that illness occurred when one of these humors was out of balance. Hippocrates did stress the importance of fresh air, a good diet, and plenty of exercise to help the body heal itself. Hippocrates's students had to swear an oath to help their patients and do no harm before they could become doctors. Doctors today still swear a modern version of the Hippocratic oath.

EARLY THEORIES OF GRECO-ROMAN MEDICINE

In ancient Rome, Marcus Terentius Varro, who was born in 116 BCE and died about 29 CE, was a scholar and accomplished writer known as the "most learned of the Romans." He came up with a concept that seems close to modern germ theory. Varro wrote that tiny creatures too small to be seen by the human eye lived in swampy areas, entered the human body through the mouth and nose, and caused disease. Another writer, Lucius Junius Moderatus Columella, also theorized that disease might come in some way from marsh insects or possibly other small creatures. But nothing really developed from these theories.

ARAB AND PERSIAN CONTRIBUTIONS

During the Middle Ages, most of the advances in understanding how to fight infection and disease came from the Arab and Persian world.

Rhazes (al-Razi), who was born in 865 CE and died sometime around 925 CE, was a Persian doctor who worked in the hospitals of Baghdad around 900 CE. Rhazes translated some of the works of the Greek doctors, such as the followers of Hippocrates, observed his patients carefully, and took precise notes. He published case studies, including those leading him to discover the difference between measles and smallpox. This marks one of the first written examples of a doctor identifying a specific disease. Rhazes's manual, *Al-Hawi*, was widely read throughout medieval Europe, and his text on smallpox and measles was still in use in the eighteenth century.

This illustration shows Persian physician and alchemist Rhazes, or al-Razi (*left*), working in his laboratory in Baghdad, around 901 CE, where he was also chief physician of the city's hospitals.

Another famous Persian doctor was Avicenna (Ibn Sina), who was born in 980 CE and died in 1037 CE. Avicenna wrote more than two hundred books. The most famous was the *Canon*, a medical textbook incorporating old and new discoveries about diseases, fevers, and remedies. Avicenna stressed the need for cleanliness during surgery to keep open wounds from becoming infected.

Meanwhile, in western Europe, many medieval doctors followed Hippocrates's idea of four humors within the human body. They also believed that disease was caused by the sins of the sufferers. Because few people understood sterilization, plagues spread easily, especially through crowded cities.

One nasty side effect of this problem was anti-Semitism. Bubonic plague, one of the great scourges of the Middle Ages, was spread by fleas and the rats that carried them. Since Jewish homes were kept free of rats, fewer Jews fell sick. The Jews, however, were blamed for the plague—because they kept clean homes.

A RENAISSANCE FOR EPIDEMIOLOGY

In Italy during the Renaissance, Girolamo Fracastoro (1478–1553) was a multitalented man: a doctor, astronomer, philosopher, and poet. He theorized that infection was due to "seeds of disease," germs, that multiplied within the body and spread through human breathing. But there was no way to prove his

THE FIGHT AGAINST GERMS

theories. Athanasius Kircher (1601–1680) was a German writer and scientist who wrote a treatise on the bubonic plague of 1656. In it, he stated that tiny animals might have caused the plague.

It was Antonie van Leeuwenhoek of Holland (1632–1723), however, who made the most significant discoveries about disease during this era. Van Leeuwenhoek hailed from a merchant family and never earned a degree from any university. Still, he was highly intelligent and had an insatiable curiosity about the world around him.

In addition, he was handy and resourceful. While working as a fabric merchant, he learned how to grind lenses for glasses and then taught himself how to make simple microscopes. He designed and built more than five hundred microscopes during his lifetime. He became so skilled that some of his creations magnified small items over two hundred times. Using these tools, Van Leeuwenhoek discovered bacteria, parasites, blood cells, and many other microscopic creatures. His research findings were widely circulated and opened up an entirely new world of microscopic life to scientists.

Antonie van Leeuwenhoek's seventeenth-century microscope was an invention that proved invaluable to the discovery and understanding of microorganisms.

CHAPTER 3

MILESTONES IN GERM FIGHTING

Now that they had the tools with which to identify their microscopic enemies, scientists could actually begin to find ways to combat the germs that caused disease.

In the eighteenth century, perhaps one of the most feared illnesses was smallpox. It was highly contagious and was especially troubling because its most common victims were babies and young children. Survivors of smallpox were often left disabled, blind, or both.

A SMALLPOX BREAKTHROUGH

Lady Mary Wortley Montague was the wife of a British diplomat in Istanbul, Turkey's capital, and a worried mother with a small son. Doctors there were trying to protect their patients against smallpox through the practice of inoculation. This meant spreading matter from a smallpox scab onto an open wound.

This mild dose of smallpox would give the patient immunity to the disease.

Lady Montague had her own son inoculated. Upon her return to England, she promoted the idea of inoculation, and people grew optimistic. But it was discovered that inoculation was not without risk. Some people became carriers of smallpox, spreading it to others even though they themselves didn't get sick. Other people died from the "weak" dose of smallpox inoculation.

An English doctor, Edward Jenner (1749–1823), working in Berkeley, a village in Gloucestershire, found that the locals, mostly dairy farmers, claimed to be already immune to smallpox. How so? They said that cowpox, a mild but related disease that most of them had already caught, gave them that immunity. In 1788, smallpox hit Gloucestershire. Sure enough, Jenner realized that his patients who had worked with cows and had gotten cowpox did not get smallpox.

But he needed proof. On May 14, 1796, he inoculated a boy (with his father's permission) with cowpox. As expected, the boy did get cowpox. Then, on July 1, 1796, Jenner inoculated the boy with smallpox. Jenner must have been terrified that this wouldn't work. If the boy died, he would be responsible. But the boy did not get ill. Jenner repeated the test twenty-three times and twenty-three times it worked. There could be no doubt: the farmers were right! Those who had recovered from cowpox were indeed immune. And there were no dangerous side effects or deaths.

VACCINATING ENGLAND

Jenner gave this treatment a new name to distinguish it from the the older, dangerous form of inoculation. He called it vaccination, a word meaning "from a cow." In 1798, he published his findings as *An Inquiry into the Causes and Effects of the Variolae Vaccinae, a Disease Known by the Name of Cow Pox*. Many people were skeptical. Newspapers mocked Jenner, publishing a cartoon that showed cows coming out of vaccinated people's bodies. But then members of the British royal family were vaccinated. That broke the resistance. Jenner received two grants, one in 1802 and a second in 1806. He did not live to see the day, but in 1840 vaccination against smallpox was made free for all babies. Vaccination against smallpox became mandatory in 1853.

Edward Jenner is shown giving a smallpox vaccine to a child in this illustration, probably depicting an event in the 1790s or early 1800s. Jenner's breakthroughs help beat back the disease in England.

At the same time that Jenner was doing his work, a German doctor, Friedrich Gustav Jacob Henle (1809–1885), was studying cells and theories of disease. In 1840, he published an article,

23

THE FIGHT AGAINST GERMS

"On Miasmas and Contagions and on the Miasmatic-Contagious Diseases." In it, he put forth the belief that miasma (vapor in the air) was not the cause of disease. Instead, he blamed carriers of disease that were actual living beings. In his article, Henle wrote, "The material of contagions is not only an organic but a living one and is indeed endowed with a life of its own, which is, in relation to the diseased body, a parasite organism." Unfortunately, though, he was unable to prove that those living things were the actual cause of disease.

Ignaz Philipp Semmelweis (1818–1865) was a doctor and obstetrician who was horrified that at the Vienna General Hospital in Vienna, Austria, on average 10 percent of new mothers died. Almost all of them died of the same disease, puerperal fever, also called childbed fever. Semmelweis discovered that puerperal fever was contagious—and that doctors were to blame. They were spreading the disease by not cleaning their hands after performing autopsies. Semmelweis started the practice of doctors washing their hands with a sterile solution before examining women and babies. The death rate promptly dropped to a little over 2 percent.

Unfortunately, Semmelweis's behavior was at times strange and erratic. He did not publish his findings until years later and sometimes insulted other doctors. As a result, he was often misunderstood or overlooked. Other doctors disapproved of him, and said as much. But even though they ridiculed him, Semmelweis refused to back down. In 1861, he published *The*

Etiology, Concept and Prophylaxis of Childbirth Fever. But stress from the attacks by other doctors began to affect him. Not long after publication of his work, he suffered the onset of severe mental illness. Ironically enough, he died of blood poisoning in an insane asylum. His contributions weren't recognized until several years later.

PASTEUR'S CONTRIBUTIONS

Next to uncover some of the mysteries of dangerous germs was a French scientist, Louis Pasteur (1822–1895). Pasteur started his career as a chemist working with the wine industry, but soon became fascinated with bacteriology, the study of bacteria. Up until that time, scientists still believed in the theory known as spontaneous generation, in which living things, like germs, could spring up from nonliving things, like earth. Pasteur proved that even microscopic creatures could come only from other microscopic creatures.

In the early 1860s, Pasteur realized that the reason that wine sometimes turned sour was due to germs getting into the wine. He found a way to kill those germs through controlled heating. Pasteur used this method to preserve milk and beer as well. The process came to be named after him and is called pasteurization.

Pasteur also solved the mystery of why silkworms were dying off (thus endangering the French silk industry). It turned

Louis Pasteur is shown here in his laboratory in an 1885 painting by Albert Edelfelt. Pasteur was a pioneer in explaining the causes of disease and creating cures for them.

out that a germ was attacking silkworm eggs. Pasteur showed silk producers that by getting rid of the germ, the disease disappeared, and became the industry's savior.

Still another of Pasteur's great achievements was showing how diseases are caused by germs that multiply in the body. He also built on Edward Jenner's work. Germs weakened in a laboratory and then placed in an animal's body helped the animal gain immunity. Pasteur used his improved method of vaccination to protect sheep from anthrax. He proved that vaccination could be used against other animal diseases as well.

In 1881, Pasteur made the last of his great discoveries. He had been studying rabies, a dangerous disease infecting wild animals and occasionally domesticated ones and humans, too. In the nineteenth century, rabies was considered incurable.

Pasteur came up with an experimental vaccine but had yet to test it. Then, in 1885, frantic parents brought their son to Pasteur. A rabid dog had just bitten the boy; he would die if untreated. Pasteur warned the parents that his vaccine was experimental, but there wasn't any choice if the boy was to survive. Pasteur used the new vaccine on the boy—and it saved his life. Rabies was no longer incurable.

Another scientist built on Pasteur's work. This was Joseph Lister (1827–1912), a British surgeon at the Glasgow Royal Infirmary in Scotland. For years, people believed that infections were caused solely by bad air. Wound sepsis—the term for a wound overcome by infection—was thought to occur when the injured area started to decompose. But so many patients were dying of what was called, for want of a better term, hospital disease—up to 50 percent of amputation cases, for instance—that Lister suspected there was something more at work. He did his best to encourage the safe healing of wounds and then tried to find a likely cause for these infections. Could it, he wondered, be the fault of some "pollen-like dust" getting into wounds?

Then, in 1865, Lister heard of Pasteur's work and made the connection between germs in the air and wound sepsis. The germs had to be destroyed before they entered a wound. He knew that carbolic acid had been successfully used to rid cattle of a disease-causing parasite, and he started cleaning wounds with a solution of carbolic acid.

In 1867, he announced that his patients at the infirmary had been free from sepsis for nine months. By the 1870s, German surgeons began practicing what came to be called antiseptic surgery, including using sterilized instruments.

But in the United States and Lister's native England, doctors weren't so approving. They disbelieved Lister's germ theory

THE FIGHT AGAINST GERMS

and wanted valid proof. On October 26, 1877, Lister carried out an operation under antiseptic conditions and made sure that operation was both witnessed and well publicized. Antiseptic surgery soon became accepted almost everywhere, nearly eliminating postsurgical infections.

KOCH'S POSTULATES

A German doctor named Robert Koch (1843–1910) built upon the work of Joseph Lister. In 1872, Koch investigated anthrax, the disease Pasteur had stopped with his vaccine. Koch studied the blood of infected animals and found the actual disease-causing germ, a type of bacteria. He published two articles, one in 1876, and another the following year, describing his findings and a way to study bacteria and even photograph them. In 1877, he also published a book listing the steps needed to learn what germ causes what disease. Scientists still use what are now called Koch's postulates:
- The microbe must be present in every case of the disease but not present in healthy animals.
- The microbe must be capable of being isolated and grown in a laboratory culture.
- After growth in a pure culture, the microbe must be able to reproduce the same disease in a healthy animal.
- The microbe must be isolated again from the newly infected animal.

Robert Koch (1843–1910) became of the most prolific innovators in the war on germs in the latter nineteenth century. Beginning with progress against anthrax, his next important discovery came in 1882, when he found the germ that caused tuberculosis. In the early 1880s, he found a way to grow bacterial cultures for study in substances such as gelatin. In 1883 and 1884, he found the germ causing a cholera epidemic in Egypt and India. The year 1891 saw Koch founding the Institute for Infectious Disease in Berlin, the first of its kind. In 1897, Koch found the germ causing rinderpest, a cattle-killing disease in South Africa and developed a cure. In 1905, he went on to study the mosquito-borne African disease called sleeping sickness. For his achievements, in 1905 Koch received the Nobel Prize in medicine.

While Koch was figuring out how to grow bacterial cultures, a Danish scientist was developing a way to classify bacteria by staining them. His name was Hans Christian Gram (1853–1938). In 1884, Gram discovered that bacteria could be divided into two classes, which he called

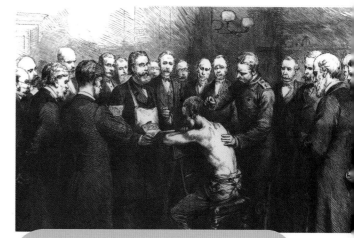

A doctor inoculates a patient against "consumption" (tuberculosis) at the Royal Hospital in Berlin using "lymph," a weakened *Mycobacterium tuberculosis*, a treatment pioneered by Robert Koch.

THE FIGHT AGAINST GERMS

Gram-positive and Gram-negative. Gram-positive bacteria have thick cell walls that stain purple. Gram-positive infections tend to cause high fever. Gram-negative bacteria have thinner cell walls and stain pink. Gram-negative infections tend to cause shock and sometimes death. Gram was a rather shy and modest man. Even though the technique bears his name, he wrote humbly, "I have . . . published the method, although I am aware that as yet it is very defective and imperfect; but it is hoped that also in the hands of other investigations it will turn out to be useful."

CHAPTER 4

THE MODERN ERA AND BEYOND

At the end of the nineteenth century, the age of antibiotics arrived. Antibiotics are chemical substances, natural or synthetic (artificially created) that destroy or restrain harmful bacteria.

Sir Alexander Fleming (1881–1955) was a British scientist at St. Mary's Hospital at the University of London. In 1928, he quite accidentally discovered the germ-killing power of *Penicillium notatum,* the scientific name of a mold from which the life-saving antibiotic, penicillin, was first purified. By chance, he had forgotten about a culture plate he had left with some bacteria on it. When he returned, Fleming was astonished to find that a tiny bit of the *Penicillium* mold had sprouted in the plate and killed all the bacteria around it. The discovery would eventually open up a new era for medicine.

THE FIGHT AGAINST GERMS

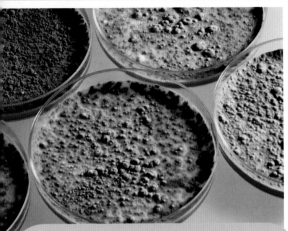

Penicillum notatum, the moldy source of the antibiotic penicillin, is shown growing here in petri dishes. Its bacteria-killing properties helped usher in the modern era of antibiotics.

It was not until 1940 that this discovery was fully exploited. Two British scientists, Howard Florey and Ernst Chain, found that penicillin protected mice against a number of bacteria. This jump-started the development of penicillin for human use. It had a huge impact in saving soldiers' lives during World War II. Fleming, Florey, and Chain won the 1945 Nobel Prize in medicine for their discovery. Penicillin was available for general public use by the end of the decade.

Other researchers soon began discovering and classifying more antibiotics and their effects. Several types of antibiotics are common now: penicillins, cephalosporins, aminglycosides, chloramphenicol, tetracycline, macrolides, and antifungals. All are related but are different enough in their chemical makeup that each type can attack a different type of dangerous germ.

Living in the modern era, we forget to appreciate how well protected people are from germs. In developed nations, a visit to the doctor or dentist means being pretty certain that his or her tools will have been cleaned and rendered free of

Autoclaves use high temperatures and pressure to free items of germs. Here, a lab technician inserts surgical instruments for sterilization so that they will be clean before use on patients.

germs—that is, sterilized. Sterilization via extreme heat or even radiation usually does the trick. Even homegrown sterilization techniques—such as heating a needle or tweezers before removing a splinter—are the result of hundreds of years of knowledge and experience.

We also use disinfectants. A disinfectant is a substance that destroys germs on nonliving things, like clothes or floors. Disinfectants are added to a city's sewage system to keep it from spreading dangerous germs. They also are used in hospitals. At home, though, household disinfectants are usually so mild that plain soap and water are just as useful. There are several basic types of disinfectant. These include:

1. Alcohol: This type of nondrinkable is used, for instance, to disinfect thermometers.
2. Formaldehyde: Used by hospitals to disinfect equipment.
3. Hypochlorites: Including chlorine bleach, these are found in household detergents, as well as in sewage treatment plants.
4. Iodophors: These contain iodine and are used to disinfect large areas in hospitals.
5. Phenols: These are used to disinfect floors, garbage cans, and the like.

There are also vaccinations to protect us from disease. In the United States, Canada, and other countries, we are vaccinated as very young children against many diseases such as smallpox, polio, measles, tetanus, and others. We immunize our pets against rabies. There are four main types of vaccines:

1. Live attenuated vaccines: These contain germs that have been altered so they can't cause disease. Some examples of live attenuated vaccines are measles and chicken pox vaccines.
2. Killed vaccines: These contain killed germs. The various forms of influenza (flu) vaccines are of this type.
3. Toxoid vaccines: These contain toxins (or poisons) from the disease germs that have been made harmless. This type includes diphtheria and tetanus vaccines.
4. Component vaccines: These contain parts of the whole germ. Examples of this type are the hepatitis A and B vaccines.

A toddler receives an immunization shot at a doctor's office. A series of vaccines she gets in the first years of her life will arm her against a host of infections.

We will probably continue to see vaccinations as the best way to deal with dangerous germs, at least in the near future. It's the most practical method we now have.

A major problem is at hand with antibiotics, though. Some germs are developing resistance to antibiotics. This can happen through mutation. Mutations are changes that occur in the germs' genetic material, or deoxyribonucleic acid (DNA). This can also happen from the transfer of DNA from one germ to another, creating a new, drug-resistant strain.

THE FIGHT AGAINST GERMS

One of the biggest reasons for these changes has to do with the misuse of antibiotics. Not every disease needs to be treated with antibiotics or can be treated with them. Two main types of germs—bacteria and viruses—cause most infections, but while antibiotics can kill bacteria, they do not work against viruses. And it is viruses that cause colds, the flu, and most sore throats. Just the same, every year, antibiotics are given to treat illnesses that can't be cured by them. This exposure to antibiotics that can't kill them gives viruses a chance to mutate and grow stronger. The same thing happens when a patient is told to take an antibiotic for ten days, yet stops after eight because he or she feels better. Then only the weaker bacteria will have been killed. The stronger ones live on. This creates a stronger breed of germ.

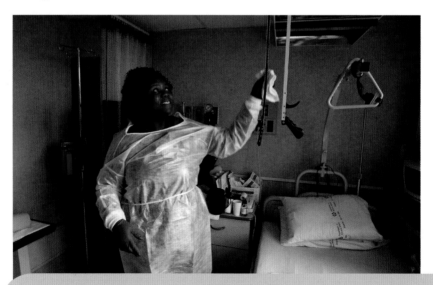

A health professional at the Miami VA Healthcare System sterilizes a hospital room to minimize the risk of a contagious *Staphylococcus aureu* bacteria strain passing among patients and medical staff.

Another possible problem may be the use and overuse of antibacterial products such as soaps and detergents. There's no real evidence that using a germ-killing soap at home does much good. Instead, those products belong in hospitals.

There are concerns that creating an environment that is actually too clean and sterile—whether it be at home, in schools, or elsewhere—may be making the current generation of children more susceptible to worse infections in the future by taking away from them the hard-earned immunity they may gain from minor exposures to germs in the natural environment.

Similar worries abound regarding antibiotics. Their overuse could actually end up making infections worse than before. Scientists agree that there must be more careful use of antibiotics and equally careful study of any drug-resistant infections. There must also be more research into the ways that germs fail to respond to drugs so that new, more effective drugs can be developed.

Still another problem is the use of antibiotics in our food. Antibiotics are sprayed on agricultural crops for disease control. Antibiotics are also used to treat and prevent diseases in food-producing animals, as well as to improve their growth rates. Critics worry—and many biologists now agree it is a valid concern—that widespread use of these antibiotics on meat later consumed by much of the public may weaken not only humans' immune systems, but may also give rise to new superbugs that could do tremendous damage.

DNA AND DISEASE PREVENTION

In April 2003, the leaders of the international scientific project called the Human Genome Project announced they had completed their mission: to sequence, or identify, all the genes of the human body. With this and other genetic research continuing through today, the possibilities for exploiting knowledge of human DNA to fight illness are endless. One possibility for fighting disease-causing germs in the future may be drugs that are designed to match a patient's DNA and specific characteristics. The idea is called personalized medicine, also known as individualized or precision medicine. In the future, everyone may carry special genetic-profile information cards. Then, if someone falls ill, the information card will give doctors the data to prescribe a precise and accurate treatment for that person. Doctors will theoretically also be able to provide preventive treatments since detailed genetic information will provide clues as to what kinds of germs and illnesses patients are susceptible to as well as what kinds of treatments will work and what kinds may actually harm patients. While practical methods of such treatment have yet to be rolled out, many researchers are confident that they will arrive sooner than expected and revolutionize medical care.

A scientist holds up a gel readout of a process that completely catalogues individual DNA. Such information may provide individualized treatment against bacteria and other germs for patients in the near future.

What diseases will be cured in the future can't be known. Whether new or mutated germs will cause new problems is uncertain, too. But one thing seems certain. Germs have been around for a long time. In the future, there will still be helpful and dangerous germs. And there will still be scientists who make amazing medical discoveries.

GLOSSARY

ANTIBIOTIC A substance that can destroy or inhibit the growth of germs.

ANTIBODY A substance made in the body that destroys or weakens germs.

ANTIGEN Any object in the body that triggers the human system.

ANTISEPTIC Refers to substances or procedures (like surgery) which are designed to ensure that infectious germs do not grow and/or are killed.

BACTERIA A category of single-celled germ, many of which cause illness.

HUMORS Substances in the body once believed by ancient scientists to determine human health.

IMMUNIZE To medically treat to prevent infectious disease.

INOCULATION Treatment with a serum made with bacteria.

LYMPHOCYTES Another word for white blood cells, the immune system's microscopic warriors against disease.

MICROORGANISM A living creature of extremely tiny, microscopic size

PASTEURIZATION The process of heating to kill bacteria; the name comes from its discoverer, Louis Pasteur.

PENICILLIN An important antibiotic made from a type of mold.

PERSONALIZED MEDICINE Also known as individualized or precision medicine, this is a possible branch of future treatments that may rely on a person's complete genetic record.

PROTOZOA Single-celled organisms with nuclei, some of which can cause illness.

STERILIZATION The process of cleaning objects of potentially harmful germs, using cleaning products or radiation.

SUPERBUGS Powerful germs that may develop in the future due to overuse of antibiotics.

UNICELLULAR Tiny organisms whose bodies consist of just one cell.

VACCINE A preparation of a weakened or killed disease germ that gives a body antibody production against that disease.

VIRUS A type of germ which acts as a parasite that invades and replicates itself within other organisms.

FOR MORE INFORMATION

Canadian Foundation for Infectious Diseases
The Hospital for Sick Children
c/o Dr. Susan Richardson
Room 3654 Atrium
555 University Avenue
Toronto, ON M5G 1X8
Canada
(416) 813-5990
E-mail: cfid@researchid.com
Website: http://www.researchid.com
The Canadian Foundation for Infectious Diseases (CFID) seeks solutions to better understand, diagnose, control, and treat existing and emerging infections that threaten public health.

The Centers for Disease Control and Prevention (CDC)
1600 Clifton Road
Atlanta, GA 30333
(404) 639-3534
(800) 232-4636
Website: http://www.cdc.gov
The Centers for Disease Control and Prevention (CDC) is the primary United States government agency in charge of tracking, treating, and prevent public health threats, including infectious diseases.

National Institutes of Health (NIH)
9000 Rockville Pike
Bethesda, MD 20892
(301) 496-4000
NIHinfo@od.nih.gov
Website: http://www.nih.gov

The National Institutes of Health (NIH) is a research facility in the Washington, DC, area that is the primary agency of the United States government in charge of biomedical and health-related research.

The World Health Organization (WHO)
Avenue Appia 20
1211 Geneva 27
Switzerland
Website: http://www.who.int/en
The World Health Organization (WHO) is the specialized agency of the United Nations that is primarily concerned with international public health.

WEBSITES

Because of the changing number of Internet links, Rosen Publishing has developed an online list of websites related to the subject of this book. This site is updated regularly. Please use this link to access this list:

http://www.rosenlinks.com/GDCO/fight

FOR FURTHER READING

Asher, Dana. *Epidemiologists: Life Tracking Deadly Diseases* (Extreme Careers). New York, NY: Rosen Publishing, 2002.

Clark, David P. *Germs, Genes, & Civilization: How Epidemics Shaped Who We Are Today*. Upper Saddle River, NJ: FT Press, 2010.

Gaynes, Robert. *Germ Theory; Medical Pioneers in Infectious Diseases*. Washington, DC: ASM Press, 2010.

Herbst, Judith. *Germ Theory* (Great Ideas of Science). Minneapolis, MN: Twenty First Century Books, 2013.

Hyde, Natalie. *What is Germ Theory?* (Shaping Modern Science). St. Catharines, Ontario: Crabtree Publishing, 2011.

Hude, Margaret O. and Elizabeth H. Forsyth. *The Disease Book: A Kid's Guide*. New York: Walker & Company, 1997.

Jakab, E.A.M. *Louis Pasteur: Hunting Killer Germs*. New York: McGraw-Hill, 2000.

LeMaster, Leslie Jean. *Bacteria and Viruses*. Chicago: Children's Press, 1985.

Patent, Dorothy Hinshaw. *Germs!* New York: Holiday House, 1983.

Smith, Linda Wasmer. *Louis Pasteur: Genius Disease Fighter* (Genius Scientists and Their Genius Ideas). Berkeley Heights, NJ: Enslow Publishing, 2015.

Willett, Edward. *Disease-Hunting Scientist: Careers Hunting Deadly Diseases* (Wild Science Careers). Berkeley Heights, NJ: Enslow Publishing, 2009.

Willett, Edward. *Infectious Disease Specialists* (Extreme Science Careers). Berkeley Heights, NJ: Enslow Publishing, 2015.

Andrewes, Christopher Howard. *The Natural History of Viruses*. London: Weidenfeld & Nicolson, 1967.

Asimov, Isaac. *How Did We Find Out About Germs?* New York, NY: Walker Publishing Company, 1975.

Brown, Jack. *Don't Touch That Doorknob!: How Germs Can Zap You and How You Can Zap Back*. New York: Warner Books, 2001.

Bryan, Arthur H., and Charles G. Bryan. *Bacteriology: Principles and Practice*. New York: Barnes & Noble, 1960.

Buchanan, Estelle Denis, and Robert E. Buchanan. *Bacteriology*. New York: Macmillan, 1951.

Gaynes, Robert. *Germ Theory: Medical Pioneers in Infectious Diseases*. Washington, DC: ASM Press, 2011.

Gillies, Robert Reid. *Bacteriology Illustrated*. Baltimore: Williams & Wilkins, 1973.

Gradle, Henry. *Bacteria and the Germ Theory of Disease*. Charleston, SC: BiblioLife, 2008.

Knipe, David M., and Peter M. Howley, eds. *Fundamental Virology*. Philadelphia: Lippincott Williams & Wilkins, 2001.

Kurstak, Christine, and Edouard Kurstak. *Human and Related Viruses*. New York: Academic Press, 1977.

Tierno, Philip M. Jr. *The Secret Life of Germs: Observations of a Microbe Hunter*. New York: Anchor, 2002.

INDEX

ABOUT THE AUTHORS

Margaux Baum is a young adult nonfiction author from Queens, New York. She has written numerous books for Rosen Publishing covering disease prevention, drug addiction, and science.

Josepha Sherman has written everything from fantasy novels to science book to short articles about quantum mechanics for elementary school students.

PHOTO CREDITS